The Beautiful Moment of Being Lost

Also by Michael T. Young

Living in the Counterpoint
Georgetown, KY: Finishing Line Press, 2012

Transcriptions of Daylight
New York, NY: Rattapallax Press, 2000

Because the Wind Has Questions
Brooklyn, NY: Somers Rocks Press, 1997

The Beautiful Moment
of Being Lost

Michael T. Young

POETS WEAR PRADA • Hoboken, New Jersey

The Beautiful Moment of Being Lost

Copyright © 2014 Michael T. Young

All rights reserved. Except for use in any review or for educational purposes, the reproduction or utilization of this work in whole or in part in any form by electronic, mechanical or other means, now known or hereafter invented, including xerography, photocopying and recording, or in any informational or retrieval system, is forbidden without the written permission of the publisher:

> Poets Wear Prada
> 533 Bloomfield Street, Second Floor
> Hoboken, New Jersey 07030
> http://pwpbooks.blogspot.com

First North American Publication 2014
First Mass Market Paperback Edition 2014

Grateful acknowledgment is made to the following publications where some of these poems first appeared:

> *The Blue Unicorn, Broken Plate, The Chaffin Journal, Clark Street Review, Common Ground Review, Heliotrope, Jellyroll, Lily, Lips, The Louisville Review, The MacGuffin, nycBigCityLit.com, Oak Bend Review, Plain Spoke, Poem, Rattapallax, RATTLE, The Rockford Review, Rosebud, The Same, The Sow's Ear Poetry Review, Spillway, Sweet,* and *Truck.*

Many of these poems were also published in the chapbook *Living in the Counterpoint* (Georgetown, KY: Finishing Line Press, 2012). "Where Dragonflies Sleep" is forthcoming in the anthology *The Bug Book* (Hoboken, NJ: Poets Wear Prada, 2015).

ISBN-13: 9780615971100   ISBN-10: 0615971105
Library of Congress Control Number: 2014903079

Printed in the U.S.A.

Front Cover Photo: A southern Maryland turf farm at sunrise, 5/30/2009 5:50AM, Nikon D40, © 2009 Charlie M. Wrenn III
Author Photo: Kaitlyn Chow

For Chandra
with whom every moment is a beautiful moment
even when we are lost

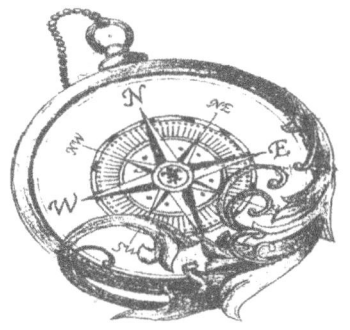

Table of Contents

I

The Risk of Listening to Brahms	5
The Word "Anyway"	6
The Continuous Thread	7
How the World Might Seem to My One-Year-Old Son	8
Broken Glass	9
Ransom Note	10
A Method of Escape	11
Textures	12
Evidence of Exile	13
Kidney Stones	14
Autobiographer	15
Slug	16
But Instead	18
Hesitations	19
Nocturne	20
Where Dragonflies Sleep	21

II

Pocket Holes	25
Honeybees	26
Reluctant Histories	27
The Butterfly in the Gutter	29
The Hospital of His Wounds	30
Counterpoint	31
Cloud Shadow	32
Descriptions	33

A Virginia Landscape	34
Passage	35
Salt	36
Weighing In	37
Crickets	38
The Unearthing	39
Against the Current	40
Just an Idea	41
As Though	42
Keeping Time	43
The Closing	44
Passacaglia	46

III

The Beautiful Moment of Being Lost	49
Directions	50
Destinations	51
A Parade of Sails	52
Announcing the Stops	53
Nightlight	54
Parallel Paths	56
Fully Immersed	57
Eyewitness	58
As Is	59
Adjusting the Instruments	60
Frames	61
Domestic	62
Sudden Snowfall	63

Zero Knowledge	64
By Returning	65
Undigested	66
Distinction	67
Writ in Water	68
Fish, Salt and Sanity	69
Like Bells	70
Acknowledgments	72
About the Author	75
About the Cover	76

The Beautiful Moment of Being Lost

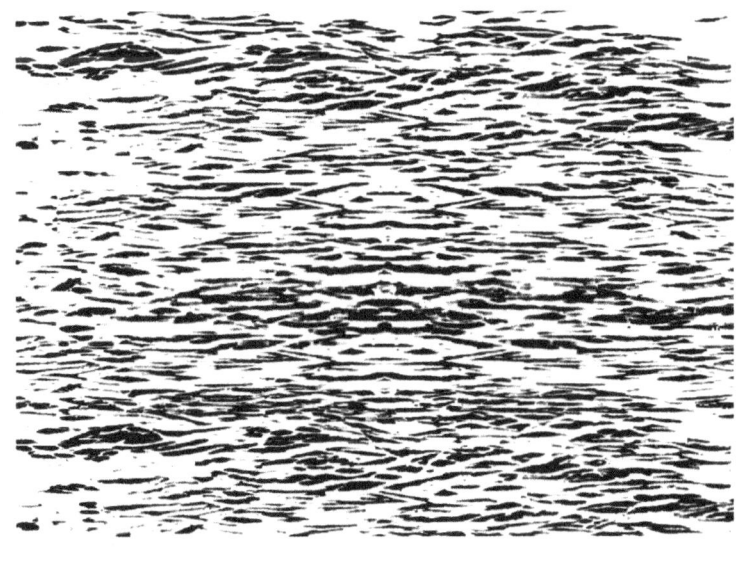

The Risk of Listening to Brahms

I like action movies for the same reason
I like Brahms, or undiluted scotch,
the constant flux of the sea,
or the sun's light and heat stripped down
to raw fire, to the burning sine qua non,
like the first time I fired a gun and felt
deliriously naked and in that denuded moment,
remembered what I was chasing after when
as a teenager, without telling anyone,
I hopped on a bus for Philadelphia
and checked into the first hotel,
struggling to dodge those who knew me
to find if I wasn't something more
than they expected, or could become
something other than they could know,
thrilled by the risk and uncertainty, the same
as when I hiked a mountain without water
on a humid summer afternoon,
trudging deeper into heat exhaustion,
the nausea stopping me every twenty feet
to gather strength from the pleasure
of wondering if I would make it home.

The Word "Anyway"

Every time I write it's there at the end of my paragraphs,
so much so, my friends see it as a kind of signature word,
and I realize that whatever it means, it is, in any case,
like a ramp off the highway leading me somewhere else.
And where it takes me, regardless, turns and carries the letter,
the conversation, the e-mail, in another direction, though not,
necessarily, in a better one — the detour this time taken
to wrench the heart from its daily obsessions,
which is to say, I wasn't trying to take us to our destination faster;
on the contrary, I was trying to spare you,
trying to take us both somewhere neither of us had been,
a place where the view over the valley
gives way to a lake reflecting late summer light
and the crisp air in our lungs expands
like a space we allow each other to become whatever we wish.

The Continuous Thread

One thing leads endlessly to another.
Even if this street is a dead end,
it will continue in a different fashion:
houses with backyards lost in a shade of maples,
a modest suburban wood — or even a wall,
and on the other side, a private deck,
or maybe an alley. It might be the one
taken to avoid the class bully when young,
and not just a single time, but days and days,
going the longest way home till it became
a way of thinking: finding the most circuitous path
to explain those inconvenient thoughts,
chattering to friends, filling those gaps
that circled the center of a labyrinth
where no one could understand
and the terrible silence was closing in.

How the World Might Seem to My One-Year-Old Son

The whole world is the given, free
everywhere and dangerously possible
like a bruise, a bump on the forehead,
the ever-out-of-reach — a computer, a bathroom —
mysteries that tall people inhabit briefly,
then return, pleased with themselves
having known the fruit of the undeniable.
They offer it to me only as fructified
in these shaky steps I take, these legs
nearly paralytic, this mouth inarticulate
as one chewing gristle, lurking near
the sinister, which surprises, puzzles
and even astonishes when it grows
into the Gauls invading Italy for a glass of wine
or Napoleon unshackling the last
of Medieval Europe with an imperial hand,
after having lain prone, subject, sometimes
even naked, simply waiting for a chance.

Broken Glass

A shattered bottle glitters on the sidewalk,
fragments dazzling the spring light
into a mesh of fence wire, a hazy net
in the warm air, like everything submerged
under the wash of memory,
caught in the refracted temptations
rising against Mother's warnings:
"Don't play with the broken glass,"
"Don't touch the fire." An undertow
tugging from childhood, tapping my hand
away from the gas stove, or calling to me
from the back door as I kneeled in the alley
holding a shard up to the sky.
And in that same era of warnings,
I cut my hand on a sardine can
while trying to tear the key off
because I was fascinated by the idea of a key,
this instrument, like a password or secret language
that could open the way into some hidden place,
a place like the wound itself that left no scar
or a gleam rising from a fresh cut, a drop
glittering like a fragment of carnival glass,
the flush color of the antique vase
I remember tipping from the top shelf,
because all I wanted was to hold the sunlight,
to take in hand the dangerous brilliance
balanced along the edges of each jagged piece.

Ransom Note

Afternoon in late August. You see it on everyone's face:
in the park they're all thinking of summer's end,
the warm flesh and greens that follow its tunnels
down into the cozy murk, how the fountain spray
pushes back at the sky, sunlight inches southward,
and even finches thread the air as if to catch something,
to cage it, like me, knowing that for all the mystical courage
of remaining silent, I have no nerve for it. Even now,
where I sit on the bench, shade slips over me like a hood,
and I'm whisked off, abducted by the day's closing minions,
the cool, the unwinding, and then a rising in the gorge
to shout my existence back against the burning gyrations,
repetitions I struggle to evade by sitting here in the park
puzzling over this stooped woman and young girl
ferreting through the garbage for discarded cans and bottles,
evidence, even when damaged, that something got away.

A Method of Escape

Whenever we go for a walk you ask
where we are going and I think,
Eventually, where we started.
So let the time between be unplanned,
as uncharted as the charted urban streets will allow:
stumbling into the street fair on Hudson
or stopping for a beer at the Blind Tiger.
Never let the usual expectations plot the course,
they will come without our help: hunger,
exhaustion, foot pain. This time,
don't anticipate the contingencies,
leave the umbrella in the closet, wear sandals
even though a stone will sometimes get in
and poke your heel, don't bring a book.
Take pleasure in running for cover
when it starts to rain, or in letting yourself
be drenched by the summer downpour
as you wander streets dreaming up
an intricately plotted novel you will never write
because its characters are clever enough to escape
the limits of any world you imagine for them.

Textures

Odd that hearing your own voice
played back on tape
should sound like some vulgar version of oneself,

its repetitions like an accusation,
that nothing changes,
that old habits never die. Odd, especially,

since echoes return like an answer
to some unspoken wish,
as though the fascination of an echo

lies not in hearing one's own voice
repeat the stale and familiar,
but in the texture the sound gathers

traveling through the hollows
of wood and stone,
so like a young man sent off

to study in a foreign country,
it returns to tell stories
that will change your life.

Evidence of Exile

My goatee reminds no one of the Devil, but rather professors and beat poets. Thus the nether worlds of Hieronymus Bosch conjure no homesickness but instead the attitude of aesthetic distance, a scholar who later stands at the head of a class discussing "Howl." Is this choice? One image suggests another, thus associations snowball or rather storm as if sunlight thickened to the density of ice crystals, drawn out like clouds distended into a funnel, a whirl, the tornado that will reassemble the house into a ruin of potential. That is to say, a flurry of connections that so resemble wreckage one questions, *Do people think this of me because I wear glasses or because of the absence of a tail?* Eichmann too wore glasses and didn't have a tail. So why should the way my eye sometimes drifts remind no one of Sartre and my love of coffee not place me at a French café? Exiled before it was completed, Marie de Médicis had the palace of Luxembourg built to recall a moment growing up in the Palazzo Pitti in Florence. Today a tourist photographs its garden paths to store in an album as evidence of the difference between choice and necessity.

Kidney Stones

They push out with a pain compared to childbirth.
So I think of them as bearing some parental likeness,
an enduring, harder part of me
calcified in the visceral dark.

The doctor wants lab tests to determine
if they're made of calcium oxalate: a mineral trace
of my passion for spinach and beer, or maybe
of my gastronomic sin of drinking too much coffee.

But I wonder instead if these are evidence
that my dear habits are turning me into stone
and if so, is there in them anything of my love
for Bach's music or long walks with no destination?

Every day something escapes me, a little at a time,
and I seem less myself, as if I were being chiseled
into a monument, the dross swept from the studio floor,
until what's left is a statue to someone like Perseus,

who once dodged being turned to stone by Medusa's gaze
only to be turned into paint, marble, bronze
by centuries of artists paying tribute
to someone who never existed.

Autobiographer

He wrote and lectured on his life
to escape invention, to reach
down the throat of event
into the minutiae, grip
the simultaneous shards
of each moment: what sock choice
on a Monday morning
scotched his promotion, or what
loose thread in his collar
turned him down the alley
where he cheated on his wife.
But he couldn't tell enough of himself,
or the world, to escape story and plot,
so that one day he just stopped
in the middle of the sidewalk
and looked down, staring
as if he'd lost something so small
he didn't prevent anyone passing by
from treading it underfoot.

Slug

I nearly stepped on him in the half-light,
but caught myself. Then I turned to watch him
gliding through the evening shadows.
His long, slick body curled — spotted brown and white —
eye stalks glistening.
        In the dim glow —
part streetlight, part moonlight —
he only turned his head,
seeming to consider which way to go.

Watching his deliberate movement, I forgot
he was a name we give each other in contempt.
What I noticed was his strange beauty and slow power,
and what in me refuses to be rushed,
doing one thing at a time, carefully,
like scraping the pots clean of dried pasta,
or writing the same poem over and over,
till every word is the right word, the right word.

And here's what always found a place to think —
a place alone at a lakeside, on a hill, by a window.
It's what liked thinking from the start,
pursuing its own light on long walks
till it could see meaning in a line of trees
or the degrees of receding rooftops,
a glint in the black tiles, a sheen on the red tin,
a meaning that was never final, only changing,
a kind of movement that began in my earliest thoughts
growing up among the hills of Pennsylvania,

listening to wind in the winter trees,
or crickets on summer evenings, their trill
filling the bedroom where my sleep came easy.

But Instead

To wake, to hear rain,
to hear drops break
on screens, on leaves, on streets.
To be thrust from dream
no hint emerging, but instead
to linger by windows,
to smell wet petals,
to recall some moment
so old, so yellowed, so scented,
it brings to mind a book,
a passage, a theme,
a point to it all.

Hesitations

There is always waiting,
not for the usual arrivals
 — the bus, the bell —
and not in the usual places
by the door or under a window,
but where the rapid's violent praise
grinds the river stones,
or steam from a sewer grate
ghosts the morning street.

I hesitate at my entrance, for its clatter,
its contagion, the odor of its meaning.
These equivocations are a kind of respect
for what was here before I came,
a hope to see what winter maples
snag in their surging limbs,
or hear the voice in light
whose only utterance is melting snow.

Nocturne

A January night, and snowfall
covered a darkness deeper than the snow itself.
I waded through the icy drifts
while the wheels of passing cars
slowly dredged the depths,
silently dragging wakes of whitened soot.

At home, you waited,
thinking of what I couldn't imagine.
What I remembered
was how the night before my father died,
it snowed like this: large, heavy flakes
like small, cowled shadows
falling in their dark silence, and I realized
that every day is like this one,
that even on the brightest, warmest days of July,
I'm walking these rising, white mounds toward home
where you wait in the habitable light.

Where Dragonflies Sleep

Our last day in the French Quarter,
a brass band off Jackson Square
played "When the Saints Go Marching In"
just as the waste of sunlight beaded and burned up
across rooftops and in the spire of St. Louis Cathedral.
Bells tolled and the day sank into earth.
Night came first as dark clots in the oaks.

While the last blue still held the upper air,
in fissures of each cracked wall tile or in the slate
flagstones that buckled like colliding icebergs,
a flash of iridescent power settled
as if all the dragonflies in the city
had come to rest in these imperfections.
The force and buoyancy of their wings
fanned subterranean fires and stoked the air
till currents banged a wind chime
made of a brass doorknob, the gas lights
budded and blossomed into fire
and electric ticker signs buzzed and beckoned
toward the center of the thundering weathers inside us
where, however small, those powers sleep.

II

Pocket Holes

The vine clinging to the window
has withered to a loose network of gray spines.
In the yard, brittle brown leaves dry
and click like husks when the wind blows,
spinning as if they were brief storms
of weathered scarabs, veined garnets,
relics of the summer past mixing with remnants
of bark and maple, hedge and lawn.
Pressing my hand to the glass
I see it as a similar bony reminder, a token
suggesting that failures of memory
ripen object into artifact, as today
the teeth of an electric saw tear through the solitude
punctuating the late afternoon air with a thud,
distant voices instruct the carving and hammering
of wood into post, sounds similar to those
when columns were chiseled for the Parthenon,
or stones in the Via Appia were tapped into place,
the early morning labors, bruised fingers
paving the difficult path down centuries,
all feet traveling the long, hard way
of misplaced pendants, amulets slipping
through pocket holes, falling to the roadside mud,
lost and slowly encrusted with the age and rust
that now glitter in the dim light of our museum casements.

Honeybees

I feel myself change, simply walking
into shade along a street; I come suddenly
upon the scent of snapdragon or hear
a distant car crash and find my every thought
stalled at the gate. And when I read
that honeybees are dying in thousands,
an epidemic no one can explain, I wonder,
Have I forgotten something? Who am I now?
There are theories, there are whole histories passing away,
but I can't describe them. So, from the next table,
bits of conversation break into my soliloquy;
or my neighbor's phone rings through the walls,
and I join a dialogue with a stranger. To call any of it
a change of scenery or costume is to misunderstand.
The world is not a stage, and the honeybee
is not the soul it once symbolized. This is why
I'm fascinated by bricked-in windows,
old tenement buildings throughout Jersey City
with their view closed up, so I wonder
what life used to be like there, daydream about who,
on a hot summer day, leaned on that sill,
breathing in the confusion of car fumes and flowers,
himself daydreaming until his elbows ached
and he remembered there was a clogged drain
in the bathroom, and so turned back,
pausing for his eyes to adjust to the dark room.

Reluctant Histories

Through the open windows
we heard dry leaves grate the macadam —
sound of water, sound of fire arguing the source of autumn.

The season's chill was taking over
while we sat inside drinking scotch,
the flavor of aged leaves, the complex color of decay.

The heaters clicked at the baseboards
and we toasted my first book, or was it the sale of your
 childhood house? —
your father two-years dead, the tokens of an earlier life being
 auctioned off.

It was night and the four of us
went outside to argue over the stars,
your oldest friend convinced that the brightest wasn't a planet.

It hadn't changed position in over a month,
lingering by the moon and Pleiades in its course, like him,
hovering by his window each night, the brightest star in a small
 town,

perhaps the last. We went back inside
mourning and celebrating, consoling and condemning
at the same time, because biography is history, because in
 another hemisphere

the stars are all different and even there,

no matter what you drink, or how much, you can't forget,
and that doesn't change, and the other side of the globe is always
  out of sight.

The Butterfly in the Gutter

My infant son grasps his pacifier,
brings it to his mouth, pulls it away.
Impulsively he repeats the motion,
growing frustrated
because he hasn't learned to let go,
to put the pacifier in his mouth
and leave it there.

Do we ever get good at this, the letting go?
Think of the many nostalgic hauntings,
past lovers shaking their purses
full of perfect imaginary coins of what
it used to be like, let's say, with Tina,
my first kiss in the alley behind my aunt's house
or moving to New York without a job
or a place to live, just hopping on a bus
on a July morning in 1990,
trusting everything I believed in then
to make a way and actually finding it,
so now it's recalled as a cherished golden age,
which, at the time, promised nothing more
than the light that falls here in the park
among the flowers, grass and dirt
where a monarch butterfly takes off
to settle instead in the gutter
and run its feelers over something,
studying to discover its worth.

The Hospital of His Wounds

I take a kind of nourishment from water sizzling in a stream
or autumn leaves boiling in the street as wind stirs the pot.
I am a body sustained by lean meats, consoled as I wait
to see what remains after everything I'll forget
and have forgotten. It will be a natural monument,
like a canyon or mountain, something weathered into existence
by the slow powers of erosion and subterranean pressure.
Although, even now certain gorges and passages take shape.
For instance, that night at about 2:30 a.m., a jagged wailing
as if a newborn had been bludgeoned by a blackjack
startled us from sleep to find a possum in the dogwood
and a raccoon testing his boundaries, like me with memories,
wondering what kingdom they circumscribe, and my role there,
and why I should be tickled to recall your fascination with roadkill,
or why I can't forget a crow that pinned a pigeon
and pecked the meat spilling from a wound in its neck,
and now a headline that has never left me, which read
that a man was "in the hospital of his wounds." I remember
thinking how, by this odd syntax, he would convalesce
in strange pulsing rooms, deep in his lacerations and bruises,
healing at the root of marrow and lava and memory,
halls and corridors that could not be photographed
like anything of real passion but where he would wake
as the first man to know who he was without looking back.

Counterpoint

In the cemetery at the end of the block
there is a stone for Musico.
And I think how this harmonizes
with other disjointed rhythms —
my glance out of tune with the daylight
so I have to look twice to clearly see the name,
my sense of vertigo when I turn back
and feel the speed of the passing cars
just off the sidewalk, and later that night,
our misunderstanding, naming the constellations,
disagreeing about the visible hemispheres.
It's by such dissonance I know
that I am dying in my rhythms,
but living in the counterpoint:
that someone will wake up fifteen minutes late,
while I wake before the alarm goes off,
and looking out the window, watch clouds
change colors in the morning light.

Cloud Shadow

If it comes over me without my noticing
it's because the source is so remote.
How imagine a spirit this downcast
gathering its folds like a darkness
far from my daily considerations
and the harbor lights it later would dim?
All news is local, like the morning traffic,
arguments with the landlord, a leaky faucet.
While my father sat determining
what last thing to tell me before he died
this shade pillar thickened over the Atlantic
darkening the troughs of blue reflection,
a depth distended from a high blown mass,
a body resembling a drift of creased bone.
Yes, a cloud, and simply fascinating,
but less disturbing than its ghost
walking the earth, this presence arriving
like the end of birdsong, altering the texture
of the most familiar streets, as if the trees and cars,
the houses and people there were composed,
given significance by the deliberate artistry
of Cézanne or Degas — a painting or pastel
with its date and name on the museum plaque
legible at a glance, even as the lights go out
and the last visitors are turned away.

Descriptions

I recall hearing my dead friend's voice and try to describe it,
saying, "It was like someone scrambling through channels on a
  radio,"
or "It was like someone pumping car breaks."
But knowing you never heard it,
I turn to other memories, also unique,
like seeing color on my parents' black-and-white TV as a child,
the scent of wet pine needles in the Pennsylvania mountains,
a street in New York, a cemetery in Paris.
And if I go on describing things like this,
it's only because behind them
there is something else the words can't describe
and sometimes, from the other side of a poem,
when I turn around to look at what it said,
what I see aren't the words, but the outline of this other thing
like a solar eclipse, beautiful, but blinding to look at.

A Virginia Landscape

A free people claim their rights as derived from the laws of nature. — THOMAS JEFFERSON

Fire burns behind the walls of this weather: morning clouds smolder the fields, threading gray light through the gold, dry grasses of January. A confusion of warmth melts the evening rain. The shed's red siding smokes. An oak's bare branches lurch into the winter air like an insight, an epiphany of wet bark, under whose protective arms all the puddles release their smallest reflections, their briefest or dimmest impressions of passing hubcap, cat's tail, late autumn leaf and every bird that gathers to drink.

Passage

The cellist next door practices at night.
His fingers summon Bach suites
in a series of movements.

These remind me of a theory
that matter is composed of strings
jittering at various speeds.

So I know the difference between wood,
plastic and metal for the same reason
I can distinguish Bach from Mozart.

Not music but motion — and no rest
in a universe that moves me to tears,
where sleepers dream, and I wake

to find my head on the keyboard,
the letter I was writing to you
trailing a scroll of P's down the page.

Salt

I like to think of Lot's wife not looking back,
but going on to another city with her husband,
Hebron maybe, or Gaza, even a small unknown town,
where she gives birth to two daughters and a son,
lives in a house with a vineyard and a view of the sea.
Though not for faithlessness of its people,
they have to move again, tread the long miles
to some new polis in the foothills. In time,
it too will send them packing, like the next,
though each place keeps them long enough be called home,
where she falls asleep easily and wakes to familiar smells,
yeast in the crock and goats in the street,
from kindling to ashes, seedtime to harvest,
comforting cycles that begin to recall earlier days,
such as the one of their arrival here,
or the day they met their friends who, tonight,
invite them to dinner, and whose faces
will be remembered with the many other cities and faces
they've had to leave, the memory of each
salted like meats packed for long voyages.

Weighing In

The ancient Egyptians believed
that when someone dies
the heart is weighed against a feather,
and for a soul to go on to peace
it cannot weigh any more than this.

"As light as a feather," we say
for a load that's effortless to lift or carry.
But also when the boy wants to impress the girl,
carrying all her luggage up the five flights;
he'll ache for three days without complaint.

Although, the gods aren't so easily fooled,
and slipping a twenty to Thoth,
who records the weight of the heart,
won't work, since they are incorruptible
and eternally honest. Or perhaps

it's not that they're incorruptible
but that there's nothing they can't get.
With all the time in the world on their hands
there is nothing that won't come to them,
eventually. In the end, everything is theirs.

And the spoiled children of eternity
are fascinated and perhaps even puzzled
why, for the thousands of years
they've been weighing people's hearts,
not one of them has ever passed the test.

Crickets

The sound of crickets is the distance
between our childhoods: even one
of those saws in the dark keeps you awake,
while it sings me to sleep, and even more
pushes me up through the summer leaves
into the green dreams of youth and clarity,
when my belief in vision was harder
and stronger than the rocks in the field.

Days in the summer of 1984, I entered that field
to sit by the lake where dragonflies
strafed the reeds, mosquitoes punctured
flashes of sunlight and mallards overhead
dragged their shadows through the water.

I thought, *this is how a mind works*,
even in the dark, when bats come out,
feeding on what floats to the surface of a day,
because that is what night is:
the thin line at the top that bends light
and changes everything. For that summer
my best friend died and became
another rock buried in a field, another spot
where crickets, all night, hack, and saw,
and cut away the differences between us.

The Unearthing

With a deep knowledge of the earth,
Grandfather cracked open simple stones
revealing to me the crystals inside a geode.
He flashed black lights on coarse rocks
till their hidden radiation fluoresced
with unearthly oranges, reds and blues.
In the basement museum he displayed
petrified dinosaur teeth, Herkimer diamonds,
amethyst and fluoride, telling me a little about each,
the secret ways they were shaped in the earth.

Meanwhile, under his cap, the disease eroded his memory,
carried off particulates of knowledge, his mind
passing slowly away like a geologic age,
replaced with fossils, traces of things forgotten:
where he left the car, the sweater he wore yesterday,
his address, my face and grandmother's face,
under his eyes, all hardening into nondescript stones
and dropped down a hole so deep in his mind
none of our names could be unearthed.

Against the Current
for Adie Mitchell

My friend sat at the edge of the hospital bed
looking for her sock. She glanced from side to side
but the brain tumor wouldn't let her see it
lying between her thigh and left hand.

I came with a gift, a copy of Virginia Woolf's
The Waves, a book I'd dipped into every spring
for the past three years, comforted
by its buoyant music, its tidal humanity.

But instead of reading, she rested and I sat
staring out the window into the spring light
thinking that some part of me
was off swimming in the cold irony

of how my friend, who had helped me
understand my father's cancer, was now
dying of cancer, and if only that part
could fight its way back against the current,

as if we were slowly drowning in unawareness
and all I needed to do was concentrate hard enough,
I could rescue even that part of my friend
that was there with me in the remote waters.

Just an Idea

I am the abstract man, living life in my head. And in these halls — how little people suspect — drift the aromas of lilac and lily, the sun's burning iris diffusing its setting light through the maples and steam from the refinery smokestacks, while the crimson at the horizon shifts into fading surges of heather. It is the idea of spring and like a book opens in the mind of the reader, motionless under his lamp at night. And this is what spring will be for all, come autumn, come winter, just an idea, a memory or hope, maybe of gratitude.

As Though

Hunching toward the cold of my thirty-sixth winter,
I watch the slow preparation of months gathered and sorted,
cleaned and stored. It is all laundry as I stoop to the floor
to pick up yesterday's socks, then pause at the window
where maples and mulberries fling their own summer laundry
across our backyard lawn. Wind tumbles and spins
the yellows and maroons in a wash of chill air,
then drops them back to the frosted grass
in a confusion of tie dye and paisley.

Now the trees are bare down to their threaded branches
where abandoned nests hang like lint caught in a cotton gin.
On the ground, squirrels root through a waste
of parsley and marigolds in the garden plots
as though these brick bins
held the satisfaction of their fastidious hunger.

Keeping Time

Fired into existence in dark furnaces
far from the light and air it now bridges,
an origin of molten metal, distillates of wood —
coal and peat — flexed into these arcs and curves,
the Pulaski Skyway defines space and time as a trajectory
that I now follow along Route 1&9, my car
spanning rivers and factories, pipes
and smokestacks jazzed by the piano keys
rising and falling from the radio.
The sweep of the bridge, a brace of girders
bolted and tarred against the wind,
the diffused morning light, a pink haze,
each element part of a chord
harmonizing New York City
into a distant silhouette, a variation
improvised from ages of light cooking the mud,
a theme that cannot be paused or replayed,
while I keep time as long as I can,
listening, watching, waiting for my exit.

The Closing

On my desk is a coil of fossilized ammonite,
an ancient mollusk curled into itself like a brown wave.
I rub its smooth, dead intimacies with my finger
and think of the sea, the splashing and posturing
tucked under each crashing breaker.

Outside the window, squirrels leap from utility pole
to hanging branch and their mid-flight poise
brings to mind a whale tunneling up through dark currents
to pierce the surface then plunge
shattering the towers of sunlit water.

Everything reminds me of the sea, of lakes,
of waves and the indifferent aqueous graces,
even the gravelly floorboards creaking under foot
radiate with grains that ripple and burn
like those in a pond pulsing from a tossed stone.

Then I read the poems of John Clare,
who saw the sea only once in his life,
and I imagine that moment, his thoughts saturated
and sinking until he believed he was Lord Byron,
crippled and swimming the Hellespont.

So I go outside where, in my riverside city,
gulls tilt over the rooftops and I stoop to the ground,
take a handful of dirt and close my fist over it,

to remind me of the shore and all those viscous fingers,
to remind me how they grope and claw the sand,

to remember everything they endlessly reach for.

Passacaglia

Shostakovich's Violin Concerto No. 1 in A minor, Opus 77 (III Passacaglia - Adante)

This river slows and trembles, a violin string
vibrating between the banks of a wartime town.
It dashes its high notes against a few rocks,
and further on, tosses an alluvial fan of sand and dirt,
artifacts and relics flung ashore,
a spindrift lifted into an orchestra of singed elms.
How it loses itself in its losses,
the evaporation of its passing, its current
throwing faint light back into the smoldering.
But nothing is forgotten, only attenuated
in the drifting dilutions of history, small drops
that wet the branches and remaining leaves.
There, in the green reticulations, the bark's crevices,
it is a thought, it is all that's remembered
and is enough for a hawk to feed on,
for men leaving their ruins to emerge on shore
and see it take to flight above the smoking tree line.

III

The Beautiful Moment of Being Lost

The secrets of a place are in its small streets,
its narrow passages, the alley in Venice
with cobblestones worn down and wet
by the humidity and dank progression of centuries,
the way we turned the same corner as others
in different years had turned into that dead-end
with its dark alcove, back doors and a wall
gaping with a niche containing a statue
of the Madonna and child, or in Florence
along a street where we pressed
into the painted brick to let a bus go by
while you pulled my backpack out of the way;
gnarled streets in Amsterdam, lower
Manhattan, passages like crooked fingers
pointing the way back to childhood,
when I liked to hide in closets, crouch
in a hamper full of clothing or make a tent
out of a bedsheet. Or the passes
and cul-de-sacs stumbled on in a beautiful
moment of being lost, the way we come
into life, without intention, snug in the primal dark.

Directions

Beside me on the train a man is reading in Chinese.
He turns the pages from left to right,
skimming characters from right to left, and top to bottom.
I read in the opposite direction, in English,
observing how our contrary motions
mirror each other's gestures of comprehension.
Our heads tilt in a slow nod or shake;
our eyes cross figures in the air
writing a tenuous language that seems to say
there is no backward or forward,
no behind or ahead, only movement
from character to character, from stop to stop,
in books, on trains, in memory — a turn, a switch,
a pattern like the recollection of a wind
quilting the water of a lake, a remembered place
where this grand gesture of air
sweeps over the surface, and reaching the shore,
without pause, passes on, losing itself
in the maple trees at the foot of the mountain,
only the smell of spring leaves lingering.

Destinations

Around this turn
the roadside drops off to the right
unfolding a long tree-lined mountain ridge,
the gradient of its green slope
drawing my gaze along its top,
a slow descent into the distance,
where, from the left, the arc
of another ridge cuts it off
with the steep swing of its sharp edge.
Beyond the V where they meet,
a valley extends,
pulling me deeper into the expanse,
luring me out through air and light,
through patches of cloud shadow on the land,
converging at the horizontal of a last mountain ridge
where my sight rests.

What is it in a view
that takes me in like this? —
the inviolable distance through which I see
the figure of one tree in a vast field
gathering all the space into itself,
gathering me, and in those branches
growing more real —
or from the promenade, Manhattan's skyline,
building clustered next to building,
catches the final daylight in its towering windows,
lifts it above the shadows crowding its streets,
and lifts me too, into its privileged heights.

A Parade of Sails
The July 4, 2000 Celebration in New York Harbor

A haze rises from the Hudson.
Gray light through the clouds
dirties the white fabric of sails:
small sloops, schooners and clippers
drifting between naval flagships.
A thread of weather angles down,
billowing the layered slopes, sheets
stretched under a displacement of pressures
propelling their glide over the waves —
a pattern of motion splitting
the river into a splay of wakes.
And this is the shape of independence,
the figure its body makes through time —
the dark water sliced and welded,
the ships roped in their own rigging,
the currents of air, the weather,
the clouds and we, the crowd,
watching from the shore,
dazzled by the beauty and grace
passing by and passing away.

Announcing the Stops

I plunge into my hard-boiled love
for the indulgence of water, its viscous churches
and coral altars. I wake to barnacles in the belfry
and bells sloshing in the deep humidity
along Kennedy Boulevard. I stretch my tentacles
in every direction, clinging to statues and fence rails,
I breathe the thick blue currents,
such as they are when I listen to Bach
or Prokofiev, sit in front of a Kandinsky
or sunlight pools on a page of poetry
and I lean down to drink.

But on the train, everyone tunnels under the Hudson,
some while asleep, some while reading,
some gripping a pole, swaying in the riptide
of their waking lives and the mind shredded
by crosscurrents of competing desires.

The conductor announces over the intercom:
"This is Grove Street," "This is Exchange Place,"
"This is World Trade Center"; and later,
when I return home, the same conductor,
like a faithful Blakean, announces the same stops,
but in reverse, as if this made them
into another world, another darkness
outside the windows, another night
with cool air streaming shells and sand
and other relics of merciful judgment.

Nightlight

A shaft of sunlight breaks through the clouds above Paris.
It drifts over the bell towers of Saint-Sulpice,
one caged in scaffolding, the other exposed,
almost ordinary with its smooth, white stone.

The shaft passes with all that is going:
cars and buses down Rue de l'École-de-Médecine,
scooters and pedestrians, the wine I sip
while leaning against the window's balustrade.

I think of my friend's stolen camera
and the trust with which he lent it;
I think of getting lost on the Right Bank,
believing I was lost on the Left,
and how a ship traveling only a degree off course
will end up hundreds of miles from its destination.

The clouds close on the drifting shaft,
the city turns gray,
and from a nearby chimney a pigeon takes off,
packing the air with the power of his rising.

I will never escape my need
for movement and light, a traveler
watching a pale column floating, the pole star,
a summer dawn scattered above a lake surface,
variations on the nightlight I needed as a child,
not because I was afraid of the dark,
nor of what I was told haunted it,

but because I needed to know
that whenever I opened my eyes
I would see something, anything.

Parallel Paths

Our shadows lengthened by the same earthly torque
that drew the dusk light on toward dark
dusting the eastern terraces of Luxembourg Gardens,
the fountain's cool ripples and reflections
slipping below the pool surface, statues
wading in the day's shifting tethers
gathered the growing shades into their arms
gesturing between parallel paths and tree lines,
nature housed in an architectural sundial
cutting the terrace's arc into segments, measures
cued to this Good Friday, the coming Easter,
the flowering spring trees, graced moments
like this one our wine's aroma scented
with the soil and slope of other regions,
other places and times remembered and toasted
as divine favor rising in our glasses, as hope
commemorated under the deepening night sky.

Fully Immersed

In spite of weather, there are moments
clouds disclose the crystal and fiber
of each disintegrating wisp, such as that day
we lay on the beach of Lake Michigan,
our heads tossed back to the angle of waves
as they slumped into the sand. But
in spite of such revelation and for all our kinships,
what did we know? The land and seascapes
shut their doors on the daylight
and everything that could not be had
compacted into the night's full moon
white with all our poor judgments and wishes.

It's the same here, in the bright light of the café:
the Baroque violin concerto over the speakers
must claw through the hum of air conditioning
and cappuccino makers and indifference.
So I devise methods of distilling experience,
downing a scotch neat or washing every dish
before gathering one piece of laundry, performing
one thing at a time so I can be fully immersed.
But in spite of my earnest philosophy,
when I sit to read Emerson's *Self-Reliance*
my neighbor turns up "Purple Haze" on his stereo
or sunlight slates the bedposts in such a way
I recall the Duomo in Florence, and again
see pigeons circling the dome in a limpid cursive,
a text I return to with happy incomprehension.

Eyewitness

> *"For we walk by faith, not by sight"* (2 Corinthians 5:7).

Crossing the Hudson on a ferryboat
I'm distracted by the sensation that the river
appears as if it should be draining, spilling
over some remote and unseen rim.
So in my small field of vision,
it seems that I am no more perceptive
than the men who thought the world flat.
Not that I trust my eyes
even with the glasses they require,
unable in my thirties to see clearly
what was evident without them at twenty.
But I would like to think, in spite of it,
that my inner vision is sharper
as if age alone could teach me the apostle's words
to "walk by faith, not by sight."
I like to imagine myself advising Argos
not to trust so much in his advantage,
that so many eyes may only multiply
the number of mirages in the landscape,
that even as we see the sun sink
into the horizon behind Jersey, physics teaches us
that it has already plunged below the mark
minutes before, and we are in a night
whose darkness has not yet descended.

As Is

Although, for a moment,
the man peeling an orange
appears to cup a mouse in his hand,
its tail dangling in a coil,
and three pigeons flying in the distance
briefly look like bubbles
glinting arcs of sunlight
as they drift down the avenue,
even before I recognize these things
for what they are,
everything is
as it should be.

Adjusting the Instruments

Somewhere in its etymology the word "mystery"
derives from another word meaning "to close the eyes."
So I wonder if there is some secret
or some significance impossible to understand
when I close my eyes to kiss you or to sleep.

The ancient Greeks thought the visible world
could not be known because it constantly changed:
seeing was even less than believing. Perhaps
that's why it's best to close the eyes when praying,
and why when I wake I still can't be sure
of any of the day's indicators: the clock,
the weather, not even the North Magnetic Pole,
which the newspaper later tells me is moving,
and in a few years could drift from Resolute Bay, Canada
to northern Russia, pulling the compass needles with it.

Of course, all the instruments will be adjusted
and my plane will still land in Charles-de-Gaulle Airport.
As we move towards summer, although the sun rises
one minute earlier each day and sets one minute later,
sometime soon we will adjust the clocks,
setting them ahead one hour in a strange ritual,
which leaves me restless for a day or two,
unable to sleep easy with this new knowledge.

Frames

El Greco could have painted these clouds,
arched and massive like the nave of some cathedral
and framed as they are by the window.
Although, the middle ground is nothing he would have known:
Manhattan's buildings topped by generators and air vents.
So the world familiar to El Greco is framed by a world
beyond his knowing, and this too is framed by another,
which I cannot hope to comprehend. And will this end?
Starlight travels forever if nothing obstructs it
and even our television signals ripple beyond the galaxy.
I ride the waves of the stone dropped into the primordial pond
ages before my birth. So the future is only this:
a light that passes beyond me and my day
to illuminate the step of someone else on another
in a universe that has, for all I know, infinite space,
and endless variations on clouds, like these,
that seem the work of a sixteenth-century painter
who never would have conceived of them
as they are today, massed above the trucks and cars
that slowly grind over the bridge toward Brooklyn,
smokestacks on the horizon discharging into the gray light.

Domestic

As we drive from the Parkway to the Turnpike
pine trees coloring the road's margins green
give way to silver-gray industrial parks.
Day thins to dusk above the winter clouds
and snow taints the light and the white billows
rising from smokestacks so they appear lilac,
odd leafless flowers, puffed violet stems
blown upward into the flurries that fall
like a shower of salt, sugar and wind,
while the pipes seem like a growth of vines
stiff in the cold and the slow edible melt of flakes.
But the reasonable mind insists
it's simply industry, refineries outside
the city limits distilling crude oils
to warm our beds and heat our water,
to light our kitchens, desks and streets
as far back as the berm of the road
where pine trees thread their needles
through patches of accumulating snow.

Sudden Snowfall
for Mila Greene

In the back seat of my friend's car
his three-month-old daughter fights against sleep
as if she will miss some miraculous event.
Her eyelids fall, flick open, drift shut.
Her head tilts forward then jerks back,
tilts forward again, leaning into
the padded rail of her car seat
like someone sinking into the irresistible sea;
while we who suffer insomnia,
and are pulled into each day by early alarms,
would gladly exchange our caffeine addiction
for an afternoon nap, except for the vigil
that must be kept on the road, the care
with which the car must be driven
through the sudden snowfall
that covers the lawns of the Colorado suburbs.

Zero Knowledge

The rim of the coffee cup and the rim of my glasses
circle spaces in which it's nothing that I drink
and nothing that I see you
still sleeping in your beautiful unconscious.
And this is miraculous, since there was a time
zero wasn't a number, when this nothing had no shape.
But now, even the clock hands slide down its elegant slopes,
a visual echo, a shape that ticks away infinity
and the infinity of things: your eyes, closed on nowhere,
the cars outside wheeling down the road,
the arc of the bridge, pigeons nesting in the girders,
and a cloudy day of raindrops
exploding in puddles on the sidewalk,
making concentric rings that endlessly open.

By Returning

If no word rhymed with another,
if this afternoon light was like
no light that ever fell through trees,
and these trees themselves
like no trees ever seen,
there would be no end
to descriptions, no end
to searching for the word
that would finally make
the landscape familiar.

If this moment didn't recall
some other moment,
my watch would never make
its next round and I couldn't
tell you what my day was like.
And if every walk I took
didn't end by returning home,
I would simply keep walking
and walking and walking.

Undigested

Pennies dissolve to water in the wishing wells, a kind of camouflage, the opposite of memory. What persists is shadow at the edge of things, debris in the gaps between sidewalk and street, door and doorjamb, cracks between all the comings and goings. Under the eaves, deep in the crevices, fillers mend and dispread, untranslatable thoughts fusing the planks, the inner machinations between floors. Basements, attics, crypts, storage for all that is truly ours: honey in the tombs sweet after centuries of pharaoh's decay, burs carried from the woods on sleeves, pollen on the legs of bees. Rooted in the dust and mud, the muck and manure of history, the blossom of an African daisy floats in a glass of water, a bit of sand in the oyster, a skip in the old song becoming part of the song, grit and gravel, what passes undigested and remains itself. It is the key that should not have been swallowed, only to dislodge in the later years of autumnal refrains. But by such metal a door was unlocked to returns and further disclosures, the aromas of decay that mimic and remake the spring arrivals, the bursting hyacinth, the rain and resilience.

Distinction

It is the moon suspended in daylight,
a drop of milk roiling in the blue,
spilling its edges into the color of summer.
It is your sandy white skin tanned by heat,
tendered by water, or deep moulins, a spume
of icy transparence, insistent waves of whiteness
spiriting birch bark into the clouds,
bleeding through the view over receding rooftops,
seen from Sacré-Coeur, or through your window
where hyacinths are buried in late snow.
It is a melt of snow raining from the pines,
a shower of snowy sparks breaking —
over the branches, over the sidewalks,
breaking everywhere into something else —
a season wrapped in scented cloaks of leaves
and decay, deer behind the bushes
nudging the limits of the territory,
the pungent odor of macadam rising
toward the woods, the moon sinking out of view,
and the darkness of afternoon rain bringing stillness,
a stillness that tumbles through us in sheets,
a bright unwinding fall, pooling the drops,
part of a private lustrum, splashing our feet
as we go out, stumbling through the downpour.

Writ in Water

Brooklyn, Boston, Paris, everywhere we go
we find our way to the cemeteries.
I read the verses that tell me how soon
I will be like them whose faint names
are barely readable above their dates
or I study the slant of a broken headstone,
imagining the sunlight sloping at the same angle.
You photograph the weathered engravings
of winged skulls and dancing skeletons,
impressions sinking into the worn marble
as if swallowed by a slow-rising tide.
But photography is deference to your belief
in preservation, second to your desire
to take a rubbing of these fading intaglios,
a practice that wears away the form it captures,
lightly chalked strokes drawn over the surface
that leave an image resembling clouds in high wind
or something seen through the current of a fast stream,
its beauty seductive as the sea, or shells
lifted from the surf that has worn them smooth.

Fish, Salt and Sanity

I walked out of my way, past River Street,
toward the Hudson, pulled by an obscure need
to stand at the riverside. I pressed into the rail,
leaning toward the morning swells, Manhattan's
mammoth buildings arched in the early mist
like the spines of some animal floating in its sleep
and I thought of waking each day,
at first into silence, then breaking into a grunt
smothered under blankets and into pillows,
the daily infancy from which I crawl into consciousness
and stretch toward the window blinds into the morning light
burning at their edges and the waste of night
that lags in the brain, ripping a gorge as wide as the Hudson,
a gulf lingering only as an indistinct hunger,
or an urge toward brinks and outskirts and shores
like this one where the odorous mix of fish, salt and sanity
churn in the flux and effusion, where the waves
slosh and pound its many hands into momentary prayer,
blessing the divine debris of its body, its persistent
resurrections and endless salting of the air.

Like Bells

At a construction site on the waterfront,
light from the setting sun shifts through the building's ribs,
its steel skeleton flanked by cranes.
I pause in my homeward rush to stand at the lip of the Hudson
and watch the water reshape the same sunlight in its roil and tilt,
molding something like an architecture: dark, reflected circles
well and collapse, cables stretch and snap,
the briefest connections made between light and shape,
shadows and building girders, men hammering
and the noblest ideas we might hope to have,
which is why Socrates was a stonemason and Jesus a carpenter,
and why, as the sun falls below the horizon
and the construction workers begin to leave,
the tools on their belts clang like bells calling me home.

Acknowledgments

We extend our thanks to the editors of the following publications where some of these poems first appeared:

Blue Unicorn	"Adjusting the Instruments"
The Broken Plate	"Announcing the Stops"
The Chaffin Journal	"Parallel Paths," "Pocket Holes," "The Unearthing"
Clark Street Review	"Evidence of Exile," "Just an Idea"
Common Ground Review	"Nocturne"
Heliotrope	"Slug," "Sudden Snowfall," "Zero Knowledge"
Jellyroll	"Autobiographer," "Ransom Note"
Lily	"Nightlight"
Lips	"Domestic"
The Louisville Review	"Honeybees"
The MacGuffin	"Like Bells"
nycBigCityLit.com	"As Is," "Broken Glass," "But Instead," "Destinations," "Eyewitness," "Hesitations," "Passacaglia"
Oak Bend Review	"The Butterfly in the Gutter"
Plain Spoke	"Against the Current," "Fully Immersed," "A Method of Escape"

Poem	"Fish, Salt and Sanity"
Rattapallax	"The Continuous Thread," "Directions," "A Parade of Sails," "Textures," "Writ in Water"
RATTLE	"Cloud Shadow," "The Risk of Listening to Brahms," "The Word 'Anyway'"
The Rockford Review	"Descriptions"
Rosebud	"Keeping Time"
The Same	"As Though," "The Beautiful Moment of Being Lost," "By Returning," "The Closing," "Crickets," "Frames," "The Hospital of His Wounds," "Kidney Stones," "Passage," "Weighing In"
The Sow's Ear Poetry Review	"Salt"
Spillway	"Counterpoint," "Distinction"
Sweet: A Literary Confection	"Undigested," "A Virginia Landscape"
Truck	"How the World Might Seem to My One-Year-Old Son"

"Keeping Time" was runner-up for the 2008 William Stafford Award. "The Unearthing" was winner of the 2005 Chaffin Poetry Award.

We would also like to extend special thanks to all the people who have offered their encouragement and advice, including Barbara Elovic, Jack Greene, Roxanne Hoffman, Dean Kostos, Richard Levine, Phil Miller, Martin Mitchell, Mark Nickels, Hilary Sideris, Eric Yost, John "Jack" Edward Cooper, and Chandra Young.

About the Author

Michael T. Young was born in Reading, Pennsylvania. He moved to New York City in 1990. He has published one previous full-length collection of poetry, *Transcriptions of Daylight* (Rattapallax Press), and two chapbooks, *Because the Wind Has Questions* (Somers Rocks Press) and *Living in the Counterpoint* (Finishing Line Press). A fellowship recipient of the New Jersey State Council of the Arts, Young has also won a William Stafford Award and the Chaffin Poetry Award, and was twice nominated for a Pushcart Prize. His work has appeared or is forthcoming in numerous print and online journals, including *Coe Review*, *nycBigCityLit.com*, *Fogged Clarity*, *Off the Coast*, *The Potomac Review*, and *The Raintown Review*. His poetry has been published in the anthologies *Phoenix Rising: The Next Generation of American Formal Poets* (Textos Books, 2004), *Chance of a Ghost: An Anthology of Contemporary Ghost Poems* (Helicon Nine Editions, 2005), *In the Black/In the Red: Poems of Profit & Loss* (Helicon Nine Editions, 2012), and is forthcoming in *Rabbit Ears: Poems about TV* (Poets Wear Prada, 2014). His poem "Advice from a Bat" appears in the poetry tutorial *The Crafty Poet: A Portable Workshop* (Wind Editions, 2013), edited by Diane Lockward. Young lives with his wife and children in Jersey City, New Jersey.

About the Cover

Gracing the cover of this book is a detail, slightly altered, of a photograph taken by Charles M. Wrenn III, of a southern Maryland turf farm at sunrise.

Wrenn is a cartographer and amateur photographer. He lives in Southern Maryland with his lovely wife, Miriam, and has two grown sons, Andrew and Jeremy.

A NOTE ON THE TYPE

This book is set in Minion Pro, an Old-Style serif typeface designed by Robert Slimbach of Adobe Systems, and released in 1990 by Linotype. Inspired by the mass-produced publications of the late Renaissance, but with a contemporary crispness and clarity not possible with the print machinery of that era, even by the best of the Renaissance typographers, this modern-day interpretation is well regarded for its classic baroque-rooted styling and its enhanced legibility. One of the five or six most widely used typefaces for trade paperback fiction published in the United States over the past several years, Minion Pro is the typeface adopted by the Smithsonian for its logo. The name Minion is derived from the traditional classification and nomenclature of typeface sizes; *minion,* the size between *brevier* and *nonpareil,* approximates a modern 7-point lettering size.

www.ingramcontent.com/pod-product-compliance
Lightning Source LLC
Chambersburg PA
CBHW031207090426
42736CB00009B/817